Let's Explore

Mc
Graw
Hill
Education

Contents

A Sap Map

Pam can see a sap map.

Pam can see the  .

path

Pam can see a .

man

Pam can see a .

pail

Pam can see sap.

Pam Can See

Pam can see a  .

pot

Pam can see a  .
potato

9

Pam can see a  .
cup

Pam can see the  .

soup

Pam can see the .

people

Tap the Mat

Sam can see a mat.

Sam can tap the mat.

Sam can tap the mat.

I like the mat Sam.

Tap the mat Sam.

I Am Pat

I sat at the .

table

I can see the mat.

I like the  .

toast

22

(background) iStockphoto/Getty Images, (center) RTsubin/iStockphoto/Getty Images, (inset) Nicole S. Young/E+/Getty Images

I like the  .

pie

Nicole S. Young/istockphoto/Getty Images

I am Pat.

We See Tam

I am Tam.

I see Pam at the .

swing

I see Sam at the  .

table

I see a  .
cat

We like 🦋.

bugs

Tap, Tap, Tap!

I see Sam at the .

lake

We like the  .

lake

We see a  !
bug

34

Can a  tap?
bug

Tap, tap, tap!

A Sap Map

DECODABLE WORDS	HIGH-FREQUENCY WORDS
Target Phonics Elements **Initial and Final Consonant _p:_** map, Pam, sap	a **Review:** can, see, the

Pam Can See

DECODABLE WORDS	HIGH-FREQUENCY WORDS
Target Phonics Elements **Initial and Final Consonant _p:_** Pam	a **Review:** can, see, the

Tap the Mat

DECODABLE WORDS	HIGH-FREQUENCY WORDS
Target Phonics Elements **Initial and Final Consonant _t:_** mat, Sam, tap	like **Review:** a, can, I, see, the

I Am Pat

DECODABLE WORDS	HIGH-FREQUENCY WORDS
Target Phonics Elements **Initial and Final Consonant _t:_** at, mat, Pat, sat	like **Review:** can, I, see, the

We See Tam

DECODABLE WORDS	HIGH-FREQUENCY WORDS
Target Phonics Elements **Review Letters _m, a, s, p, t:_** am, at, Pam, Pat, Sam, Tam	a, like, see, the, we **Review:** I

Tap, Tap, Tap!

DECODABLE WORDS	HIGH-FREQUENCY WORDS
Target Phonics Elements **Review Letters _m:_** Sam; _a:_ at, Sam, tap; _s:_ Sam; _p:_ tap; _t:_ tap, at	a, like, see, the, we **Review:** can, I

HIGH-FREQUENCY WORDS TAUGHT TO DATE
Grade K
a
can
I
like
see
the
we

DECODING SKILLS TAUGHT TO DATE
Initial and final consonant *m*; short *a*; initial *s*; initial and final consonant *p*; initial and final consonant *t*